Don't Suffer In Silence

The Spiritual Remedy for Life's Worries

Carol Allgood

Published in 2012 by FeedARead.com Publishing –
Arts Council funded

Wise Owl Books

A CIP catalogue record for this title is available
from the British Library.

Contents

Acknowledgements

Allow Their Light to Shine, The Many Souls Who
Have Helped This Book Become Thine.

May Their Teachings Be Shared By Us All.

That Many May Grow From Within And
Feel Connection Once Again To Their Own True
Selves.

For All Of Those Who Will Never Be Found Lingering
At The Gate - Allow Your Hearts To Fly.

Only Then Will Your True Level In Life Be Reached -
You Will Then Sense That You Have Truly Lived.

Try And See Whether You Can Reach Out And
Touch The Sky.

Especially To:

My Great Sons who have been my rocks:
Baz and Tel.
My very Precious Granddaughter, Georgia.

Lorraine, my wonderful daughter-in-law for her much
appreciated love and support.

For Janice, my wonderful sister-in-law, for her love, warmth
and generosity of nature.

My Mum and Sisters: Barbara, Shelia and Jean - all have in
some way shared this Journey.
To all of my nieces, nephews and their siblings. Also Dave
and Tony - thank you all for being you.

I would like to thank many friends, including Lesley and
Sarah - also Lesley and Collette.
I would like to acknowledge: Jean Gallyer, David Hunns and
John Clarke for their help in the outcome of this book.
Also, Michael Meredith - I thank you.

My special thanks to Tania Cheslaw for all of her hard work
and contribution in bringing this book to its fruition. Thank
you for believing in me.

Remembering Roger - you gave so much in so many different
ways. We Love You.

And to those I have met throughout my lifetime: Thank You.

We are all wayfarers.

About The Author

I started my life in the East End of London just after the war.

Life was a struggle and this is where I started to experience emotions of my own and of anyone I came into contact with. This continued throughout my life and I found myself seeing a different dimension to what most people just accepted.

I have travelled and lived in many parts of the U.K. and spent some time abroad. Whilst undergoing these journeys I have witnessed our constant companion called Emotion - in all capacities - at work.

I grew up in a single parent family with other siblings all very different in their own right.

I have been married and divorced - each experience full of its own teachings.

I have birthed two children and share a deep unconditional love with them, which I believe has helped me to recover from any emotional disturbances I may have experienced since their birth.

I have met many other people who have shared with me their stories.

I am indebted to the many who I have known.
Without them this book could not have evolved.

Dedication

I would like to dedicate this book to my late father.

Although I spent very little time with him throughout my lifetime, each time we were in each other's presence we underwent a major learning.

Our love for each other never diminished and it grew into an ever deeper understanding. We always shared a far greater awareness of each other in overcoming obstacles that appeared to be blocking our path, until our last time spent together.

Even with a speech impediment - following a stroke - he was able to express to me that his latter years were spent in deep thought. He stated: "I have found myself."

He was 87 years of age.

I am now beginning another part of my journey towards my own self-discovery and this part, I am sure, will bring a lot of joy to all who share the journey.

The rewards are always to be found in the eyes of others. Look ever deeper for the inner knowledge, and be sure to see the reflection of your own love shining back at you.

Always remember to say "Thank You" for the time shared discovering yourself.

In love and light,
Carol xx

Introduction

I would like to share my interpretations of the emotional energies that affect us all throughout our lives.

Hello to you!! I do so hope that these words can help you in some way. Our lives are full of a multitude of emotions... they form the foundations of the many decisions that we have to make.

Having lived a life where emotions have dominated my very existence, my thoughts turned towards the prospect of trying to somehow break down the barriers that prevented me from exploring the negative side of my own human nature.

Emotions are so powerful and to override them takes an enormous amount of self-control. And this I hope will help, in some way, to lead you to a far greater understanding of yourself.

I have probed deep into my own emotional levels and have found how complicated our lives can be.

I have undergone a deep, internal analysis, in order to disentangle myself from the debilitating energies that controlled my life.

So, these findings are my own deductions from my own self-healing process. There may be those though who have also looked deeper into the emotional process and their realisations and thoughts may be in conflict with what I have deduced.

I believe that we have to learn more about this side of our human nature.

The inner conflicts that control the human race can be a very powerful energy.

And I believe that every human being desires peace at some stage of their life.

I just hope that somewhere in these words is the **Key** that will help you to turn your life towards a more peaceful existence.

Dreams

Dreams - illusion or reality?

As human beings we have inherently developed the knowledge to create our own destiny.

This requires each and every one of us to be responsible for our own soul's journey throughout our lifetime, although we are not aware - at any given time - as to where our life journey will take us in our search for the alchemy that will lead us towards destination unknown.

As we grow and mature, our awareness becomes more astute about life's complexity and we tend to also become aware of the fact that life is just not straight forward - it can feel at times like watching a ship at sea as it tilts and topples. It is also not strange to feel as if we are constantly ascending and descending to different imaginary heights, at different times.

All of these varied fluctuations encourage our minds to generate many thoughts with regards to the many unknown mysteries that coincide with us.

Whilst trying to make sense of what makes no sense at all we engage in many revelations - many thoughts about the possible outcomes of the different occurrences that life gives to us.

We have a powerful tool called the mind; our life and mind are constant companions - sharing many real - or if we choose to fantasise - *unreal* experiences.

The mind remains loyal and relentless during its tireless search through the creation of the many thoughts that gestate - whether real or unreal.

Always ready to action and process a chain of any possible opportunist thoughts in itself - it has an amazingly artful way of encouraging us into action.

All of this thought activity allows access and pro-activity, as we process the various multitude of different thought combinations. If, by choice, we allow our mind to relax into a dreamlike meditative state, we enter into a different sense of our own reality.

As the mind seeks to explore these different combinations it can become entangled in trying to decipher and understand what is really going on.

At any point there are times when we run out of enthusiasm and just want to give up and move on, but something inside of us rises up to encourage us to continue; our own curiosity instinctively wants to find out what it is that attracts us and keeps us motivated.

Emboldened by our own natures, we start to investigate what could possibly be the outcome of our thoughts; our individual mind adventures.

The many thoughts that are processing themselves through our consciousness can be evaluated and are questionable; they help to make our inner awareness more capable of coming up with well-informed choices and decisions.

The many wonderful aspirations that we have involve the by-products that our minds are quite capable of producing.

Our minds help us to assimilate a far greater understanding of what we as human beings are capable of achieving.

Our own participation can and will enable us to generate enthusiasm in order to fulfil our wishes and desires.

Our dreams are the creation stage of our reality.

But not all dreams become part of our everyday life.

Some dreams are dismissed, as they are unachievable.

Other dreams fall by the wayside, laying dormant until maybe they are brought to life at another time - but they sadly may be dismissed again.

Our thoughts are always proving to us that they are a powerful energy that can seriously help and assist us throughout our lifetime.

Consider life as a journey full of insurmountable challenges that we have to encounter and overcome - but if we are all truly in touch with goodness and pure initiative this will automatically alert us to the fact that our own mind is our natural mentor.

Just imagine that collective, positive dreams from everyone's mind could be collated and then heighten the awareness of us all by increasing our positive energies.

This could be the way forward for all human beings that evolve on earth!

Some who generate positive thought-forms could help the human race overcome our many frailties.

This could invoke a true sense of emotional belonging, and give a feeling of common unity and like-mindedness. In turn, this would have a true effect on our universal mind and alleviate concern for the future generations.

The Universal Laws of Cause and Effect are a very powerful force, and if we all were actively involved, in some way, in enhancing our own thought behavioural system, we would be engaged in a life-changing experience. This would then encourage the growth of a more positive attitude and sensitivity towards all ways of life.

Looking for ways to Create and Support the multitude of dreams and inspirational thoughts for us all could possibly have more impact on what we are all trying to achieve:

OUR TRUE POTENTIAL.

Is this just my dream? Or could this, one day, become the reality for us all?

*

Life is a mystery but, in its wake, there is always a miracle.

Emotions

What are Emotions?
Do they really exist or do we create them?

Emotions, in the main, are very much part of the integral unity of the human race.

We live, breath and evolve in a powerful, emotional energy force.

This unseen force seems to have no boundaries.

No one person can be totally separated from some form of this emotional vacuum; we all, in some way, experience this chaotic, mysterious power that can dissolve and disassemble any organised notion and throw us into total chaos.

Every day we deal with life in an emotional way and we are constantly being encouraged to interact with the many various and, as yet, undiscovered contemporary parts of ourselves.

We may become debilitated by our own emotions at various times in our lives; it may seem as if we are dealing with an alien force, intent on making us feel wretched.

We watch and we listen to others that we admire and they may also be going through a very similar experience - but it is never quite the same as our own.

5

We hear others say, "I understand", but how can they when we do not truly know or understand ourselves?

We may be reluctant to find out what is really the cause of our discomfort, as we might not want to probe too deeply – just in case we set off on another train of thought.

Such further thoughts may trigger another emotion that could make us feel even sadder!

We may become drained of energy, not knowing why.

We may find at times that it is very hard to stay focused and positive.

We need constant reassurance that we are loved and belong.

We hurt. We get angry. We laugh. We cry. We are in a constant flow of emotional energy that can and does manage to undermine what we know of ourselves and that energy is very capable of bringing about total disarray and confusion.

But then there are many other times when the world seems like a wonderful place; we feel full of joy and uplifted emotionally - then we are in a good place.

When we feel like this, everything goes to plan and we are aware that others are also smiling and in good spirits. No matter what life has to throw at us we are able to cope with whatever situation is at hand.

Our whole demeanour changes and we feel upbeat; full of optimism and our body language is open and confident.

At these times we can and do enjoy a different sense of well-being and we feel that life has a lot to offer and will support us in our endeavours.

We look forward to the future with optimism.

We are full of energy, and can deal with whatever life throws at us.

But, in some instances, this can be short-lived and life can seem like a roller coaster.

Without knowing why, our moods can change within the space of a few minutes.

This sudden change could have been brought about by anything, including a remark that might have been made to you or you could have been witness to a disturbing event. Likewise, somebody might have spoken out of turn or you may have read something that jarred within you.

These are just examples of how quickly our moods change. Our moods and their emotional complexity affect our everyday life. And because of the amazing rate at which our moods are liable to change, we can and do end up feeling emotionally drained.

These constantly changing emotions seem to have a life of their own. They are like the tides of the oceans - ebbing and flowing and, in some instances; they have no rhyme or reason.

There are many theories as to why we are affected by our own planetary solar system - but will we ever truly know?

Emotions are one of the common denominators that binds us all together, but no one can answer this:

Why do our very powerful feelings sometimes overcome us totally?

These emotions can be so very destructive and there may be times when we recoil and demonstrate an utter sense of disbelief at what is going on around us: i.e. when we look at the world news on television.

How can we feel so much emotion when viewing an event happening thousands of miles away from us, to people we have never met?

Is it because the human race is tragic and set only for more demise?

And do we have the right to be so joyful and happy when there is misery being metered out to our fellow man?

Emotions are a true mystery, but they can be beautiful – they can affect us and move us in many life-changing ways. Even though they may sometimes be out of our control, emotions can guide us onto new roads and stretch us in our endeavours.

*

A milestone in life is when you know that you have achieved your goal.

Words

Words cannot change the way we feel, but they can help us to understand ourselves a little bit more.

When we make a connection and start to look at the meaning behind the word this then becomes a Word in Action.

The meaning and the Action of the words are a powerful source of information.

They can trigger an emotional reaction which, in turn, encourages us to start to explore our own emotional feelings.

We are, in effect, already programmed with this information and by setting things in motion we can then begin to assimilate our own emotions.

By changing what we understand of ourselves – we change the way that we react to others. This self-discovery then enables us to connect with parts of ourselves that we have been unaware of; beginning the process of our own self-change.

Thus, only by accepting that we have a responsibility towards ourselves, do we then start to manifest the desire to investigate what truly makes us function as human beings.

It would be wonderful if we had the answers to our own complexity - which is part of our own physiological reasoning. We would then perhaps have more of an understanding of what a human being is and what being human really means.

We need to be able to connect and feel that we belong.

The human race is amazing but we are constantly being torn apart by wars and disagreements and that is not helping our unity.

We are meant to be able to live in a support system that generates a more positive attitude. One that will inspire the here and now. One that will afford each and every one of us the opportunity to feel motivated enough to engage in mind-provoking experiences. We need to be able to share our knowledge and wisdom with others that want to accept it. We need to maintain that wisdom and know-how for generations to come.

But if we are to make a truly great mark then we must ensure that the healing starts here.

*

A great pleasure in life is to see a twinkle in another's eye.

Learning

Learning is not just about academic subjects. It's about using the tools that are part of our everyday life.

The learning process begins from day one – our birth.

We have so much to understand about being a part of this earth and, as the decades evolve, the more advanced learning unfolds. For some, this can prove to be a very long road but others take to it like ducks to water.

So what divides the one from the other - apart from material factors and place of birth?

The art of learning is not taken seriously unless one has an aptitude for what one is being asked to understand.

All lessons should represent something that could be useful in one's life.

But much in the academic world has taken over from what we require as a human race to function. This can have a marked affect on one`s own emotional growth. We need our emotions to grow, take shape and form and help us to forge ahead and upward.

When we are very young we are expected to undertake and absorb the majority of the learning that we will need in life.

There are many other factors, such as parental involvement – parents also need to actively encourage and invest time in their child's social and developmental skills. This encouragement will enable the child to have confidence in their own ability and, in time, become part of the backbone of society.

True talent in an individual would hopefully be recognised during the course of their life and they would be encouraged to develop; regardless of their background or upbringing. They would also be shown how to impart their knowledge and prowess to the rest of society.

If a younger person is struggling to integrate, through lack of skills and emotional stability, then other factors would be looked into.

Such factors might have had a detrimental impact and have been responsible for the child's inability to achieve. One would be encouraged to look deeper and there might be other factors affecting the child's progress.

If a child is part of an environment that is affectionate and loving, he or she will grow up with this knowledge and be able to integrate with other children more easily, and, in turn, help other children to attain their goals.

Nurturing plays an important role in all of our lives but if there is a lack of emotional stability it can have a negative influence on the very essence of how we perceive and decipher other people's opinions.

If we are high in confidence and self-esteem we should be able to overcome any form of emotional abuse - but if we find ourselves in a deprived situation – a situation in which our emotions are not being taken seriously, then this can lead us to feel very low in spirit. Having a more positive outlook on life can prove to be very difficult at times.

There are some children and adults who have an ability to stand apart from others.

You may hear comments about such people and how they differ from others.

Because they shine from the inside they are able to endear themselves through their own levels of confidence.

Yet another child who is constantly seeking attention may not receive the recognition he or she deserves because they become instantly recognised for disruptive tendencies, in their eagerness to show that they also have special skills.

These children may attract the wrong attention in their desperation to be recognised.

What these young people may lack are the skills to integrate. As their insecurities surface their emotional behaviour can become more demanding on the people who are trying to teach them.

Then there are the other children who are equally as talented but are unable to showcase their gifts, due to low self-esteem and a lack of confidence. This may have been brought about by a lack of caring or in a multitude of other ways.

We can see this lack reflecting in their body language and by them not having learnt the correct way to show their emotions. They have yet to develop themselves and emerge from the comfort of their own emotional chrysalis. They may find it very difficult to believe in their own self-worth. And they may feel uncomfortable becoming involved in different activities that highlight their vulnerability.

What this pinpoints is that emotions play a large part in one's learning throughout life.

The knowledge that they are loved can help any individual to overcome any difficulties that may present themselves during a lifetime.

Emotions play a major part in our lives, but do any of us truly understand them?

Emotional dysfunction can be responsible for many of us withdrawing from society and, as a result, people become disengaged from normal, everyday courses of action.

At some stage during their growing years they could have possibly been forced by others – or by themselves - to make difficult emotional choices. They would not have been aware that those decisions would have a powerful adverse affect on their emotional structure, later in life.

If not recognised by society these persons will become negative and may form an emotional *virus* that could infect others. This virus would be subtle but it has the capability to disintegrate all that we as humans consider to be acceptable behaviour.

If any destructive level of negative emotional energy is allowed to form and germinate it will bring about change to such a degree as to affect the human race's very livelihood.

We must then undertake to be more responsible for our own thoughts and feelings and become more involved in preparing the younger generations to be better emotionally equipped to withstand their experiences.

Rearing any child is in itself a huge task.

Although there may be lots of bravado amongst children, there still persists the understanding that having the knowledge and the comfort of a loving environment can lead to a more balanced way of life.

Just having the understanding of their deepest emotional fears helps them to form more stable relationships and enables them to cope with any situation as it arises.

This will, in turn, build a natural ability and strength that will benefit the whole family.

Life can be very stressful.

If we could only deal with our emotional side and learn to accept that everybody born into this life also has to undergo many transitions; encounter many problems (whether self-inflicted or not) and understand that everyone's journey is equally as important as anybody else's - then just maybe we will find the key to a successful life.

*

Parents are great teachers, but it's okay for you to consider how not to be as well.

Energy

You are a positive light being; a beautiful energy form that glows brightly from within.

As you grow, so does the energy, but throughout your life you are being exposed to other types of energies.

You move through energy thought waves every moment of your life and your energy attracts energy; including the waves of light from the universe.

As a light being, you enjoy being around others and give out a natural, positive outlook on life and with this attitude a great deal of energy can be used.

It's not unreasonable to expect a similar feeling of energy in return, but your energy retracts every time it hits a negative person whose thoughts are being disassembled by their energy system. This leaves you feeling drained, because more energy is going out than is coming back to you.

Unless you challenge yourself, you tend to believe that you are going through a negative time as well.

Once you realise that you are not responsible for these emotions and that you have been unwittingly drawn into another's energy field, you can release this energy.

By turning your attention towards your inner awareness and relaxing your breathing, you can let go of any thoughts that have created the unrest that you are feeling. You can then check out your physical awareness and re-energise any unwanted negative emotions - turning them into stronger positive emotions - so that you can feel yourself beginning to once again relax and take control of your own energies.

By maintaining this inner knowledge you can build up an amazing relationship with your emotional self, which will serve you well during the course of your life.

We are all born with **survival** energies; these lie deep within oneself and are commonly known as our animal instinct.

You have this in-built energy system that you can learn to rely on to help you through life.

These instincts can be responsible for you feeling a great deal of confusion about yourself.

Use these instincts to protect yourself and others; they are powerful signals that alert you to any danger.

If all thought forms were positive, there would be no reason to doubt yourself or others; but expecting life to be always positive, seems more or less impossible.

Just become aware as to why you have conflict within and feel responsible for those unwanted feelings that are tumbling around inside.

Get to know what triggers the deep inner alert mechanism and learn from its teachings.

It is important to build up your own positive thought form energy, so that your own energy can assist you in any crisis that enters your life.

You can stay balanced and also be reassured that you are engaging in an emotional field, but will be assisted by your own force to withstand any negativity around you.

The more you build up this positive outlook, the wiser you become and, even though life will give you many chances to learn, you will have a far greater understanding of what is possible - and your life will have far greater meaning.

Always remember that positivity attracts positivity.

Love

Love is the deepest, innermost feeling and it lies in the well of hope.

When you love, your desires are uppermost in your mind.

At times you may think that you love, but instead you are *desiring*.

So what truly is love?

Your ability to love is the greatest thing that you possess.

It lives within you and it grows from passion.

Passion is the fruit of love.

Love grows after you have the desire for it to grow, but when love is denied it can stunt growth; inhibiting and stopping a person from becoming more balanced.

When love is given freely it produces great wisdom and nurtures our mental, physical and emotional needs.

**When you love, you nurture; you create
solace and peace.**

When you **become** love, all is possible but your love needs light to enable it to dazzle and grow.

But when love is withheld during childhood years it creates a deep sense of longing – a need or an ache to belong.

Of course, love can sadly be misused, to - in some instances - manipulate another person.

Love is the most desired emotion but the most misunderstood.

People search throughout their lives for it, constantly craving recognition from their beloved.

When there is an attraction between two people, this can also be misunderstood.

This wonderful energy that you possess needs nurturing, so it seems natural enough to look for this in another human being; **but the seed of passion lies deep within yourself**.

Once you have the realisation that you are the key to your own self-love and once you have this deep sense of belonging within, all true love can flow towards you from many sources throughout your life.

So you must endeavour to undertake the journey that will bring you the most joy.

This joy will then marry you to the love of the universe, restoring faith.

We have a fountain of eternal life that is called the **love fountain**. It is found within and it glows from within.

If you have found your fountain of love, this nurtures love in others; faith is then restored.

Also, you will feel this love from a bountiful universe, enabling you to grow.

Never fear love, but feel its wonderful energy.

It is always there to help you through any part of your life.

Love is the greatest dynamic emotion shared by the human race and the one most valued.

Welcome this energy into your heart and then you will feel a deep sense of peace.

Love will always be a great teacher - you are the student - and together you will be able to surmount all of the demands that your life will ask of you, because, within, you have found a deep sense of knowing.

*

Love comes easy when in its truest form.

Emotional Links

So how do we become aware of something we have no control over?

It takes time and a lot of understanding.

It's very complex and can be overwhelming to undergo a transformation.

You have to try and think of things that make you happy. With these thoughts you can then begin to transform your life.

You were not meant to be struggling with thoughts that make you unhappy or emotions that are so destructive that they create problems – especially when it comes to forming relationships with other people.

From day one we are overwhelmed with information and, whether we like it or not, we are being taught a multitude of tasks.

It's all about survival, but where is the teaching about thoughts and feelings?

We can all generalise about how we feel, but it's all so complex that we tend to avoid how we **truly** feel.

Some people seem to cope better than others, but then, later on in their lives, they admit that they had been acting; just trying to survive, not being open and honest about how they truly felt.

They were unable to express their feelings and were fearful that doing so would show a weakness; they were made to feel foolish during these times.

When the sense of not belonging is ever present in our lives the feeling of loneliness is overpowering and this sends our emotions into total confusion.

Just try to be accepted by others… life does not teach us how to build relationships.

Even in family groups this can prove difficult.

Throughout life, we are always being encouraged to do our best.

Some of our endeavours fall by the wayside, for whatever reason, but still we look for the motivation that can help us survive.

It can seem like a very lonely journey, but so many people on the same journey are just as confused as to how they feel. This is why I have tried to break down and illustrate some of the energies that are felt by the majority, having myself experienced and undergone many of the emotions that tend to be a part of everyday life.

I have also had to deal with my own thought patterns throughout my life.
I remember my own confusion when I had to deal with the emotions that are constantly testing my strength.

Learning to love others and ourselves is an overwhelming desire but the most difficult to understand.

If you do not understand yourself, how can another person understand you?

So, it all comes back to oneself.

We learn about ourselves from others.

We may not always agree with other people's opinions but it helps to listen to each other. That's why it's so important to communicate how we truly feel, without fear or prejudice.

We all have different agendas, but we are all born with thoughts and emotions, and the more we can begin to understand them, the more we can evolve as the human race.

We have inherited a lot of knowledge.

Let it empower us in such a way that it shows how life can begin to be a new breeding ground for love, and trust can become part of our everyday life.

We need laughter to be heard so that it can grow the feeling that we are part of something really special.

This is where the children of the future can feel that they truly do belong.

It's so easy to take for granted the contribution of others in our lives and the knowledge they impart to enable us to live better lives.

The words 'Thank You' always express how much you appreciate the amount of effort someone has taken, and, if said in connection with a true emotion, these two words leave the other person with a feeling that they have made someone happy.

When thoughts, words and emotions are put together, they have a very powerful impact on the person or persons that are listening to them.

Always keep your own council.

Be ever mindful that you are full of emotional thoughts and feelings and that one day you will truly begin to understand the multitude of reasons as to why you are **who you are**.

*

When negativity is allowed to flourish, it grows from the thorn into the might of the spear.

Fear

Fear is a living energy.

It is also a very deep emotion, that forms from part of our psychological thoughts.

In children, fear is not as strong an emotion, unless the child has been brought up in a fear filled family.

Thoughts are very powerful and play a major part in everyone's lives - especially when dreaming.

These thoughts are a deeper part of you.

They are helping you to make decisions which can make you feel good and positive about yourself .

Then there are thoughts that are like a master magician or a virus that takes over and dissolves the thoughts into a different pattern and, before you know it, you have totally changed your happy and positive pattern of thought. At that stage, you should rise up and force the *intruder* thoughts back.

Better for you to discount these thoughts, than to allow them to manifest in your mind, where they can take over and totally wreck your intuition and imagination.

So, trust yourself by holding back this negative energy and develop the strength of mind to overcome fear.

This brand of thought may totally paralyse you into thinking that you are not good enough for most of the crusades that you undertake. So, create a deeper belief in yourself and by taking control of your thought patterns you will develop a more positive attitude. With this you can and will go forward and multiply your talents and manifest your truest dreams.

When you reach any barriers you must quickly consult your own positive thought patterns and promise to grant yourself the wishes and dreams that are lying beneath the surface of your mind, and then, at last, your mind can rejoice with your soul because you are, at last, believing in your positive energy.

Fear is a master of knowledge.

Consult Fear occasionally - because Fear can also give you information about any danger that may exist, but never let it be the master.

You are the master - he the servant.

His wishes are not your commands, it is the reverse he wishes for you, but he will test you beyond endurance.

Sometimes, to develop your growth, he teaches you the hard way, never letting up until you have mastered your own thoughts.

At times, he is relentless; repeating negative thoughts, over and over again, until you have got the message.

He creeps in when you are unaware, traps you in his vice and creates havoc in your feelings - thrice round if necessary.

Never let him get a foothold, because he will stamp all over you until you scream for mercy.

It is only by looking him in the eye and trusting your own pure energy and having faith in yourself, that you will ensure that you can, and will, be free of the never-ending trail of negative thought that destroys your life.

So, only by going forward into the unknown and risking your life pattern of thought will you be free to be your own person and realise your truest potential.

*

The powerful light that shines from within is the contrast between you and the universe.

Emotional Blackmail
and
Emotional Conflict

As part of our everyday life we are bombarded with others' opinions as to how we should live our lives. We can conjure up a feeling of failure if we do not live up to their expectations.

We are all different, but are expected to follow the same pathway; regardless of whether it is the right or wrong way.

Each person has to follow the guidelines that have been put in place and these can prove conflicting at times, but you must abide by the information that is given at any one time, because life is constantly evolving.

These guidelines are no longer applicable in some areas of life but they still continue to be used to indicate how and why things are the way they are.

This leads to separatism, creating groups of individuals who have different values, each one believing theirs to be the correct way.

We, as human beings, are duty bound to protect each other.

When working for the whole, a totally different ambiance is born; a deep sense of belonging to something so awesome that it takes your breath away.

This should not be just for the few but for everyone who is part of the human chain.

We were born to fulfil nature's way.

It's a gift that has been nurtured for centuries and we are being encouraged to raise our energies so that our future can be a far cry from our past.

When the awareness is raised of just how far the human race has travelled in the last century, then perhaps we will be able to see how misshapen our understanding of it is.

Playing a major part in the growth of something so beautiful gives us so much to be thankful for, but, for the most part, we elect not to see a wonderful work of art.

Our prayers will not change something that is so entrenched in past history.

We have to be part of a whole new thought process that can and will inspire others to think differently about their gift of life.

Memories that are full of warmth and meaning can be created, but first we have to understand what contributes towards our feelings of discontent and only then can we begin the process of bringing into our lives a new beginning.

A new beginning that can and will hold memories that have far greater meaning for ourselves and the generations to come.

Let us be a part of the healing process that has had dominance for such a long time and help others to overcome their fears.

Everything has to begin with a thought.

May you be one of the first to concentrate on the many positive thoughts that will herald in our new wonderful era.

*

Great changes come when your life moves into the space provided.

Memories

Our memories are a great asset when we are aware of the reason for them. They link us to our growth.

When we allow our memories the right to flow freely, then we work within the boundaries of our minds.

These memories are all about our growth from child to adult.

As a child, memories are not so important and we are not encouraged to think, so we do not develop an emotional link, until our actions have an affect on another being.

The action - although acceptable at earlier stages of a child's growth - in an older child may be deemed as unacceptable.

This is the beginning of a whole new learning curve and it seems that adults are always moving what can be termed as the 'goal posts'.

Adults are very confusing, but they are not to blame, as they were equally brought up in a very confusing manner… and everything is based on memory.

So, consequently, you are born into a world that is structured on other peoples' memories.

These are created from many different influences, but each person is only aware of how the occasion that made the memory was for them.

The emotional link to our memories is not always apparent, as some emotions lie dormant, while others are constantly reminding us of days gone by and how to be. Some memories are like <u>conditioning</u>, and although we are aware of this, they can be a great comfort when we need to reflect or share an experience with another person.

Depending on what was happening at the time, we can dwell on memories that are not deemed as being *nice*. These thoughts and memories can bring about a dramatic change in our emotional levels - as just one negative thought connected to an emotional pain can leave our mind spiralling out of control, until we feel totally bereft.

There could be many different reasons why you had to venture into the negative side of your thoughts, but be sure that they were not trying to destroy you.

They were just reminding you of how strong you have become.

We are not always reminded of our strengths, only our weaknesses, so memories are not always linked to praise; often criticism.

So, our feelings are always under pressure - as are our thoughts. In order to grow up into balanced, well-adjusted individuals, so many factors have to be in place – and this is why you may find that some people rebel. It's not because they think that they deserve more, it's because they may have been denied a part of their upbringing that would have given them the best opportunities to express themselves as individuals.

Each person has a part to play in another's life; it's just recognising what the other is offering you, that is the skill.

However, there is one thing you can be sure of; each person you have met has left you with a chain of memories.

But the art of life is to recognise this and to thank the other for the teaching that you have both undergone.

If you feel that you need to forgive the other for whatever negative memory they left you with, you must also find forgiveness for yourself - because you both are undergoing a life transformation.

This is not always apparent straight away, but if allowed to heal, it will leave no lasting scars.

If you can find it within yourself to apply these thoughts and emotions to your life, then you will begin to understand your true inner sanctuary and what has felt so misunderstood can at last start to evolve into being you.

*

When you're alone you do have company - your own.

Negativity

Any negativity means that your thoughts are in turmoil.

When your negative thoughts are allowed to run free, your mind is at odds with itself.

Your whole being is being emotionally tested at these times and you may feel undervalued, deprived of love or misunderstood.

Another person's words may have caused you to feel pain but, whatever the reason for your negative feelings, the whole experience can be very traumatic and you may feel that your whole world is falling apart - that you will never be of any use to anyone ever again.

During these times you may feel very alone and think that life is not worth living.

Negative thoughts are like a virus to the mind.

They can be very destructive and destroy any thoughts that contain positivity.

It only takes one negative thought to send the mind off at a tangent, bringing about a catastrophic effect, if allowed to take control - and this can encourage your mind to become depressed.

What you are actually undergoing is a transition - your mind is tricking you into losing control of your own thoughts and allowing another's negativity to become part of your thought pattern.

You may find it difficult to stay positive if the people around you are miserable and always moaning about their lives.

The human mind is a wonderful energy as it has all of your potential imprinted within its cells and each cell contains a different aspect of you. However, if that energy is threatened by another person's actions, it can mean that you have to protect yourself against unwanted influences. But there may be times when these influences are being created by people you trust - that you have great respect for and love very much.

These are the times when you may think that you are being rejected, as you don't understand the other person's motive. This may result in thoughts of being let down as your faith is being tested - sometimes beyond endurance. Your loyalties are being driven into another part of your emotional field at this point; you may have a feeling of deep sadness, and the only way you know how to deal with these emotions is to go into deep thought.

Your mind is trying to work out where it all went wrong and you are asking yourself if you were in any way to blame. In some instances it could have been something you have said, without thinking, that may have caused a lot of confusion. No one is without responsibility for words spoken that have created misunderstandings. These, in turn, may have set off a chain of events that, once again, the mind has to resolve - not always finding the answers.

A feeling of despondency then fills the mind with negative thoughts.

We are subjected to a constant outpouring of grief because the world, as a whole, is struggling with negativity and we have become very sensitive to this energy.

In some cases you may not even be aware that you are being exposed to this energy and may struggle to understand why one minute you felt very positive and then a feeling of complete devastation washed over you. You then just want to be left alone to deal with your own thoughts and a person close to you might try to help to lift your thoughts, not understanding that you need time to be left alone to discover what caused you to feel this way.

This can be a difficult time between two people, each not knowing how to deal with the situation.

Both parties should recognise the other's needs – all of the good intentions by the other may not be welcome, so a lot of bad feeling can be prevented by not allowing more negative thoughts to take over an area that is already feeling very sensitive.

Just being there, in support of one another, is enough.

Accepting that the other is experiencing whatever he or she needs to, shows great empathy and care when the mind is greatly confused by the incoming traffic of thought.

Each one of us goes through a mental pain level.

If we can begin to understand its teaching then we are progressing towards a deeper understanding of how our minds are there to help and assist us during the course of our lives. If we then develop our mind and trust its progress, we will know that not all of our negative thoughts are there to destroy our belief in each other. We will then have connected to a higher thought process, that can bring about a more positive attitude.

During your life you will encounter many people, and they will have either a positive outlook or a negative one – each person has something to teach the other if one can learn to look beyond the spoken word.

You will see that the other person is also searching for answers. Sometimes they may have set their goals too high and never reach their dreams, but they would still need positive feedback, because they are trying to overcome their fears and make their way towards a more positive future.

When you have learnt to master your thoughts; and know how to encourage the positive aspect of every action, you will see that all that happens is for a reason; we all play a part in the future of mankind. You will no longer feel a victim of negativity but will welcome the thoughts and ask the ultimate question... what are you teaching me?

*

The sun shines through our eyes when we are given the time just to be.

Teacher and Pupil

We are all teachers but we are also pupils too.

No one should ever believe that they have learnt everything they need to know during the course of their lifetime.

We are all here to learn and to teach and we chose to go through different experiences.

Not only do we have the pleasure of learning, but others can learn through us as well. We are constantly being brought into contact with others who also have a sense of purpose. Some achieve what they desire to do early in life, for others it may take a whole lifetime, but whatever your part is in the evolution of the human race, you are sure to be remembered.

History is constantly evolving.

The human race is full of noble people who have explored the potential of our ancestors and put together a vast amount of teaching that can be enjoyed, but only by putting pen to paper have they been able to pass on what, at that time, was deemed to be the truth.

But history has to be re-written at times when new information comes to light.

When we enter into this vast array of teaching, we undergo a time lapse, not expecting that, at some stage in our future, we will have to go through a complete change in our thought processes.

We may feel let down by whatever or whoever used our intellect in such a way that we were made to feel stupid and manipulated, but there is always reasoning in every action and, as time goes by, the true understanding as to why becomes apparent.

You play an enormous role in the ongoing evolution of mankind when you elect to share this with others.

You are creating a milestone for the future, for, as history informs us - an artist of great vision has a following of admirers long after his departure from this earth.

*

Try to bring pleasure - it is far greater than trying to please.

Motives

Motives search for the alternatives of life and they find their mark by repeating themselves and then test the human mind beyond endurance.

It's like a fountain of youth being splayed onto water - you may think it is a trick of nature but it desires peace between the words spoken - like looking forward and finding out something has changed into a "matter of fact" situation.

The mind finds this hard to comprehend because it has great belief in all aspects of reasoning but, like the flow of a river meandering as and where, the human mind also travels and so may take the soul on unwanted journeys.

Men and women have different agendas and use different ways to think. Their difference of opinion creates motives, and their thoughts will lead either man or woman to change the content of their opinions to create opposition.

Thus, the seed of motive is born.

This then leads to a silence that allows both minds to rethink their intentions, during which the mind can create an impact on the other's thoughts.

When this point is reached, the thought creates reasoning within itself and then starts to justify the initial facts.

To rescue the *defendant*, the *opposition* may speak with a forked tongue so as not to expose its own desire to show where his own thoughts were travelling.

To expose the other's motive, the other thought form jumps to its defence and brings with it an exposé – designed to find the reasoning behind the motive.

In this way, both thought forms are locked in a dual of reasoning and motive. That difference of opinion springs forth from like-minded people to aggravate the mind into growth.

*

The things we truly own are our name and
our emotions - the rest are on loan.

Words

When speaking, if your words are shining then so are you.

They are your thoughts and emotions connecting together so that they can be spoken in a torrent or a whisper, but still they can have a lasting impact on anyone that might be listening.

Your precious words can be inspiring or dull, depending on how you are truly feeling at the time they are spoken.

Words can be very moving and fill your heart with either gladness or sadness, but, either way, they will have touched you to the very core of your being.

Songs are written from someone's deep emotional learning; maybe they had undergone the experience they have written about.

Poetry brings with it a deep sense of the writer's solitude and books are written about many different subjects and can be powerful. However words are brought into our lives, they all have great meaning and the way we use them to communicate is very important.

When words are used in anger, malice or idle gossip, they can do lasting damage to the person, or persons, who are being spoken about.

If you can refrain from being judgemental of another person and concentrate on building your own life skills, you will be rewarded in the knowledge that you were always respectful.

This takes great skill, as it can be so easy to lower your thought process and get emotionally involved. Other people may manipulate you by asking you to lie for them - be their alibi - because one lie spoken has to be upheld by another.

Inwardly, you know that you have lied and this can lead to emotional problems later in life. When that time comes you may ask someone to trust you, but inwardly you know that you cannot even trust yourself.

There may be times when you may have to soften the truth, choosing words carefully so as to protect another person's feelings, but you will find that most people are astute and will understand what you are doing and why.

Words have been entrusted to the human mind and you may think that you have the power to know exactly what's being thought by another person but it's only when thought becomes word that you have some idea as to what is going on in another person's mind.

Lies are a cheap way of getting what you want out of life and can result in you losing everything that you have strived for.

When being dishonest about your true intent, think again and have some respect for yourself and the others who have put their faith in you and love you.

When you speak your truth you are alerting the other person to what you would like in return - a mutual trust then starts to generate itself and true friendship can be enjoyed and cherished.

Never be afraid to speak the truth.

Truth is everlasting and, as it is being spoken from strength, it can be repeated over and over – resulting in peace of mind.

*

At sunrise, a flower will persist into opening.
Do not persist in walking in the darkness.
May your life open to the full beam of the sun.

Time

Time is in motion through seasons and years.

It is constant and it leaves its imprint as memories.

We have all been given the gift of memory and memory is all that we really own.

As time is the companion of memory, whatever you do with your time, your memory will record the event.

Your memory will always accompany you.

Whatever your life span, every moment spent is a precious gift because every moment presents itself as an opportunity to allow you the time to make the best decisions about how you would like to live the rest of your life.

A lot depends on how and where you are born, but every way of life has something to teach you, recognising that even under-privileged children have developed skills that are much in demand in the modern day world.

We have schools of learning that are only too willing to help in assisting you through the early years of study; preparing you for adult life.

However, throughout these years, the sense of time has no meaning if you are actively engaged in learning about family and friends, and pursuing other interests.

But, one day, there will come a time when you look up from whatever task you may be involved in and a moment passes between you and your memory - bringing the realisation that another five or ten years of your life have passed and become just memories.

Life is like having a bank account of time.

Whatever amount of time has been deposited in your account, make it work for you and invest it wisely.

This is all about self-interest but there will be times throughout your life that you will be drawing on the interest.

Nobody else has access to your account and you cannot take deposits out to repay later.

At any given moment in time, a gift of learning will be offered to you. Be it a large or small undertaking; accept the invitation to learn these skills.

They may have no value in your present time, but later in life will be of great value.

So never underestimate anything that comes into your life and remember that it's **your** bank account. Only you have access to the time deposited.

So be wise, make good use of it and learn from others who have gone on to enjoy their life through their own efforts.

*

Never allow yourself to be overheard saying, "If Only"
for that means you will have run out of time.

The Human Soul

The human soul is constantly searching for different aspects of itself.

During this search it meets new awarenesses - every one of them ready to take you further along the road of self-discovery.

It challenges you to take risks that are not always to your liking but can be very persistent in the need for self-change.

You will encounter times when the ideas that are presented to you do not amount to anything, but there are others that are so truly persistent that you undergo their passage - although doubt is uppermost in your mind.

To pursue these quests you are required to undergo many transitions - many of which you did not know you could achieve.

You may thus feel privileged to have been exposed to your own potential - having succeeded far beyond your own expectations.

Over the period of your lifetime, your thoughts are in constant motion, provoking you to analyse and deduce different aspects of yourself. If you approach this with humility you will be able to determine a far greater understanding of yourself.

Sometimes, the events that you are experiencing are just a catalyst to help you onto a different pathway. Along these unknown paths you will meet different persons with whom you may feel an affinity and if you take into account that these total strangers are being attracted towards you to provide a combination and union of energies - all designed to bring about an expansion of your understanding and knowledge of your fellow human beings – then you will know that these acquaintances or friendships are helping you in your search for the ongoing truth of yourself.

Some of these other human beings can remain with you over the course of a lifetime, others elect to move on in search of their own self-discovery.

There may be a feeling of being stricken with grief at this time. It might feel like a gradual, emotional, deep sense of loss.

When persons we have shared so much of our intimate self with have to move on - for whatever reason - they leave a void that feels similar to being bereaved. The magnitude of their actions becomes multiplied by your own insecurity.

Nothing in life is that final, life moves in circles and has a habit of delivering surprises by bringing others back into our lives when least expected - meaning there are still aspects of learning to be undertaken by all parties involved.

So, when someone announces that they are undertaking a mission - fill your heart with compassion. You may or may not understand their need, but will encourage them to follow their dreams.

This unconditional love helps them to aspire and reach greater heights in their lifetime and will pave the way for you to continue your own journey - all the while gathering knowledge which can help and assist you in your pursuits. You will grow stronger and wiser along the way.

As you become more aware that the natural flow of life has to undergo its own passage, acknowledge that the timing of events are as they should be, then your own life expectations can take on a totally different dimensional quality.

*

When all life blossoms, the outcome is the purist thing in the universe.

The Heart

The heart represents a symbol of love and, of course, the vital signs of our own physical health.

Our heartbeat symbolises and immortalises an inner quality that we all emotionally desire. It is also an emotional enchantment that provides us with whatever life expectations we would like to experience. The heart empowers us by encouraging us mentally, physically and emotionally to undergo many changes throughout our lifetimes.

When you begin to realise that each person's life is connected to the same force, then you will begin to accept some of the responsibility for the universe, and by doing so you will encourage everyone else (the mass) to feel and understand that a metamorphosis of change is now in motion.

Your heart is part of the mass and the beat of your heart joins with the pulse of mankind.

Every heart pulsates together to encourage the growth of the universe.

To be and feel part of that pulse encourages you to rethink the way that you live your life.

Mankind is all about energy which is created by our own life forces.

Allowing our loving energies to flow, not only helps to lift our own vibrations but also assists the world; creating a force of energy that shares the desire for change.

We are all part of the future and our connectedness to us is the secret.

Your heart is the giver of life and without it you would no longer be a part of the human race, just a part of its past.

While you are reading these words your heart is beating for you – just take a moment in time to feel and connect to its eternal beat.

There is a powerful energy that gives life, and without it the human race has no future.

What you, as a living human being, contributes in this lifetime, affects the human race has a whole.

We are all part of that whole, so if you can find it in your heart to start connecting by sending out your love - which costs you nothing - you will receive so much more in return.

May life and love lift you into the realms of all there is.

*

Your heart is very aware of time - it beats at every second.

The Divine Vision Of Death

Death is your transition towards the levels of your eternal life and it reaches out for your eternal flame.

To lose your life in its truth of form is to release you into another future.

Allowing the love of the physical to release all the moments held within shows true wisdom and, as you are part of the natural evolution of man, death is part of your everyday life. It lives in the answers you receive, bringing about the death of a question.

Every heartbeat is another seed, sowing itself for this outcome as your strength stretches you to the limits of your vocations.

Each death records itself in the seed and its crisis depends on the outcome within the seed.

We all have the knowledge that a special day in our future will arrive when we will once again be released into our spirit form.

As your life ebbs it greets the new, folding into its arms the Grace of God - the Soul - feeling the joy as your being turns towards the light, flowing gently as if on a wave of energy and a great understanding of peace and love rejoices with you.

At last you feel the real force of the life that you have undertaken to live; seeing the source from whence you took your first breath on earth - releasing the last and asking everyone to rejoice with you.

You are sharing love with all who have shared a part of your life, knowing that you are being reunited with the sublime beings that exist in the universe and your heart is flowing towards the ultimate union, as one with God.

As you flow through, your soul is expanding with the knowledge that all has been just as it was written, and you finally know that you have lived your life to the full.

*

Values of time are far greater when spent in non-expensive moments.

Thoughts - Words - Emotion - Creation

Words, when spoken, are thought in action.
Emotions empower word and thought.

Words and thoughts make a very powerful unit as every word that is spoken, first started as a thought form.

When emotion combines with the two, you have a circle of events that can have a long-lasting effect. They are history in the making and, as we are surrounded by words, they form the backbone of the human race. Without them we would have no effective way of communicating, as they appear in our daily lives from all around the world and they are in constant action. They also bring with them emotions that, if attached to pictures, will enhance the message that is intended for us.

We are all aware of the importance of words as they are the beginning of the learning process and they have the power to determine the course of our lives. We are the result of this creation because, without this process, nothing would come into existence.

I believe that thoughts start being formed in the embryo.

Unknown thoughts are very much part of the process of action when the human seed evolves and connects within the womb to begin the process of germination - powerful emotion is also present at this poignant moment.

So, the three elements are present and involved in the process of our creation.

Also empowering the embryo, while it is developing in the womb, is the awareness of sound.

At the birth of the child, thoughts, words, and emotions are in abundance.

Anyone present at the birth expresses, in his or her own way, the awesome moment when the created child is born.

At the point of birth, sounds take on a different meaning for the child; emotion is now very much part of the experience for all concerned.

Thoughts are becoming words and words are becoming emotions.

Everyone starts to pull together, with the best of intentions, to ensure that the child has the benefit of their skill and their knowledge.

Time is ever present during all of these processes and, without time, nothing would ever be achieved.

In the time it has taken you to read this passage, take a moment to send out one thought to a child now being born – as we are all part of the thought process.

One Of The Keys To Our Own Emotions

As human beings, our deep love of life creates and shapes itself into various forms of realisation.

Throughout our human lives, we are being encouraged to grow emotionally.

These different emotional feelings exist within ourselves to encourage our own self-desire to grow and develop.

We find ourselves co-creating with other human beings, searching for the balance that each and every one of us knows - without any explanation - exists between us.

We have an emotional affinity, not just with ourselves but also with the animal kingdom.

Our own natural environment can have a huge impact on our well being and, inwardly, we know that all of these factors can and do affect us emotionally.

We have developed the emotional understanding to discover and realise when our own self-growth requires further development.

Every person's emotional truth is as important as the next person's.

These various, mysterious emotions that evolve within us are constantly nudging us to believe more in ourselves and hopefully help us to discover what nature, as a whole, shares with us <u>naturally</u>.

These emotional signals are all designed to motivate us, helping us to release the feelings that accompany us as part of our everyday life.

We need to recognise and acknowledge that these emotions are designed to nurture us, and will constantly contribute towards us finding a form of satisfaction in whatever we undertake to aid our own transformation. This will then encourage us to trust and ultimately relinquish control over our deeper emotional, intellectual behaviour. For, if that is suppressed it could hinder our growth and not allow emotional integration with like-minded others, which is part of natural stimulation.

We need to engage with others so that we can work out how we can acknowledge and truly recognise their intentions.

The realisation that emotional trauma can co-exist as part of our everyday life can be quite daunting. Our understanding of our emotional behaviour is constantly being tested, as emotions fluctuate as we grow and develop.

Our emotional association is the connection to the heart and the understanding that the heart has a large affiliation with our various emotional moods is widely understood to be the reasoning behind why we tend to have such insecurities. This is even more apparent when our understanding of emotional love begins to flourish as part of our growth.

The nurturing side of our growth has an enormous impact on these various stages of expansion.

Nurturing plays an important role in our emotional development, allowing a happy heart to flourish. Nurturing also actively encourages a different sense of well-being.

Uplifting moments bring joyous thoughts that resonate and create a sense of harmonious self-discovery and these, in turn, help us to form the realisation of our own self-belief. We can then be delirious with joy and have a desire to discover a deeper sense of fulfilment and happiness.

But through our own levels of decision and choices we experience different learning curves - all designed to draw our attention to what we need to understand about ourselves. This is not always welcome and can be, at times, deeply disturbing, especially when there are other parties involved.

At these junctions in life we all have a tendency to look back and try to resurrect old and outmoded thoughts and feelings from when life was great.

Instinctively, we have been communicating with our emotional forums and this interaction empowers us and is character building as it gives us emotional strengths that help us during the times when we undergo any emotional pressure.

If emotions become negative and feel out of balance and are left unchecked to spiral out of control, this can lead to a total disintegration of any understanding of what we once believed to be our emotional outlook on life.

We may, at this point, feel that we had been emotionally deluded into believing that another person's journey through life was our own.

We all start out with emotional innocence but we slowly learn to develop and hone our emotional skills as part of our existence.

Having learnt these skills, we then discover how to exist and survive. This is when we will maybe gain an inner realisation that our life is far more intricate and requires far greater understanding.

We may become desperate to discover and resolve what has been creating emotional barriers.

During these trying times, our emotions can be likened to a barometer; they can travel up and down.

You may become emotionally drained and this is because there are so many different aspects to the emotions that are channelling through our emotional fields at any given time that we can get very tearful.

At other times it can feel as if we are releasing what can only be described as a primal beast that has been growling inside of us and it feels like this beast is pushing emotions up and down in an attempt to control the desire for self-change.

At this juncture, our inner primal beast, desperate to maintain its emotional advantage over any changes we may be considering, views with our inner wisdom which demands that we feel a different level of emotion. It may feel to you as if you are unsure but deep down you know that the time has come to move on with your life and accept the changes.

Any emotional release has an affect on our physical bodies.

These different levels of our own physical empowerment may demand that we let go of any unwanted old emotional feelings. These could have been debilitating and physically affected us in many different ways. For example, we can feel very nervous, exhausted, cold and nauseous.

There are also many other physical side-effects that can truly leave us feeling unwell.

We may have come to depend on emotional memories, although many of them were not to our benefit. We may have become reliant on other emotions, having formed an emotional attachment as a form of protection.

All of these feelings are presenting themselves because we chose to include them as part of our understanding and common sense.

We need them to help us make well-informed choices.

Emotions, in their infancy, are naive, until they become part of our total awareness and then bond and connect to our inner being.

So, any feelings of insecurity at this stage could be as a result of our own inability to comprehend that we are struggling and are reluctant to give way to what can only eventually benefit us.

*

The institution of the mind has profound affects on one's memories.

Emotional Highs and Lows

In time, we become more aware of our own emotional levels – they have different agendas but the majority, if allowed to flourish, will share our journey towards emotional peace.

At this juncture, one could find his or her self searching for solace and summoning up energy and strength in order to make effective changes to what once was self-belief. These changes may require one to conquer the primal energy that could cause a lack of concentration. This all may cause tiredness and distort our thoughts – and thus we once again can delay our emotional healing.

This constant personal quest towards our own emotional truth can be unsettling and very confusing, dependant on the individual and the emotional drive involved.

One life can change dramatically if the individual requires internal peace.

This may require the individual to mentally undertake a total realisation of the way that he or she understands their way of life.

Your inner self may be desperate to understand your soul's quest for truth and desires more time in which to do so, whilst searching for deeper inner fulfilment.

By bringing about a far deeper internal need in one's own self-belief we can encourage our dreams to be fulfilled.

Emotional Bridges of
Self-Change

As our own self-belief begins to flourish, our heartfelt wish for truth becomes more apparent, and we put our heart and soul into following the pursuits and quests that are linked to natural environmental issues - although we are made very aware that we live and dwell in the historical, fundamental habits of the old.

At this point we may have a sudden realisation of becoming more aware of our own soul, and with that realisation comes the knowledge that we are about to undertake another life-changing experience. A feeling of disquiet may follow and different thoughts surface. A feeling of excitement may also accompany the many emotions that abound; as the next quest within our own eternal gestation of life is formulated.

Our soul is looking for change and badly needs the destruction of old ways and habits.

As we journey on our quest for inner knowledge, our soul travels up and down the barometer of change; knowing that its battles lie with the old way of being and it growls every time our soul feels a vibration of growth.

The old instinctual behaviour within wants to retain the old ways, as they are easier, so it tries to convince itself that there is no advantage in changing one's life.

The deep feelings of change are ever more present and persist in pushing away the feelings that are preventing any positive emotional movement. This may result in a sinking feeling in the pit of the stomach, and thoughts may reflect the pointlessness of the situation. But, from somewhere deep within, a dogged determination comes to the surface to strengthen our resolve.

We are more than capable of feeling all of these changes in our emotional field.

A sense of relief helps us to relax, instinctively knowing that we have conquered and overwhelmed anything that could have prevented us from fulfilling our true life potential. And, as this understanding brings with it new perspectives of soul evolution, we are still left with the knowledge that we have to maintain the energy and all it takes to combat what has been tormenting us.

This can cause fatigue, and drag on our energy - because our inner emotions can be constantly duelling and questing for outcomes. Only when the duel is complete and the quest is over can we even hope for a positive outcome.

At these times of self-valuation we must find the time to reflect on what needs our utmost attention. We need to have time to be gentle with ourselves and rest. Ways to do this include taking a long soak in the bath, having a walk in the sunlight or just being in a place where our thoughts are allowed to reflect and be peaceful.

We do not have to rush; the art is to give ourselves time. We may feel that we are groping in the dark or climbing the walls - these feelings can all be part of the process of self-change.

We must go with whatever has caught our attention to be able to feel the incessant nature of the soul - but never fear its intentions because it is working with us to encourage a great outcome.

Any negativity at this stage can easily rid us of our growth.

We must learn to trust our own positive thoughts and wisdom as they will encourage us until we are back in full swing – we need to stand upright and be secure in our own knowledge.

Our thoughts can inspire us onto the next stage.

To be sure, our tears will well up for the old self and ways, as the new way is unknown.

It's a feature of the future.

As yet unknown experiences encourage us onto different levels of self-growth.

As we find the strength of purpose to overcome the indulgence of our insecurity, we will begin to understand that our self is all that we will ever know, but we will not necessarily always understand it. Our life will always be questing and this is exciting and adventurous – it makes our life feel rich with drama and intrigue – and these sensations help us to grow even further.

Our lives are part of the bigger picture in this world; very much a contribution to the love of all human beings.

We strive for eternal inner peace.

We desire a perfect haven and sanctuary where each and every one of us can personally accept that our life can be as complicated as the next person's.

Although knowing that life can be a complete mystery, full of intrigue and complexity, we need to truly begin to understand that life-changing experiences are solely there to ensure that we have a personal involvement in our own human destiny.

Any true involvement is to be found in all measures of human emotions.

If, as a human race, we could just stop to think about why there is so much unrest and disquiet and we just stop the **word - thought - form** for one minute so that all thought forms are in conjunction with each other and are at peace, then this will allow us to let a new beginning flow towards us all.

All human beings are united. We need to encourage unity so that it can thrive and nurture.

This is not about religion or politics; it is about the human race - a powerful emotional energy that has so much potential as a whole unit and it is one where optimism can abound.

If this emotional togetherness begins within many hearts and is allowed to flourish, it could possibly take us all forward into the world's next quest.

As part of the soul of the human race, we rejoice as we move into a new era of human discovery, where we can and will make a concerted effort to learn of our co-existence.

We can begin to realise and understand that there are no differences between love and hate - both emotions can create deep emotional bonding.

Emotion can be truly wonderful in the love sense but totally paralysing when any one of us is being controlled emotionally and we then feel full of bitterness and hatred.

However, both emotions connect us to another.

We are able to suppress many thoughts and emotions within ourselves, somewhere deep in our All-Knowing.

Our knowing self is like an emotional library that revolves constantly: every dimension a part of our internal awareness.

Some emotions get filed incorrectly, thus bringing about emotional confusion, because they do not belong where we have put / filed them.

There are times when our inner awareness attempts to secrete thoughts that we have shelved deep within our memories. This can, at times, create an emotional upheaval which opens up a deep void that internally can seem impossible to heal.

We may feel totally emotionally inadequate to help ourselves, and, in some instances, feel powerless to overcome our own emotional thoughts and feelings and **be** what is most needed.

We all learn to engage with others in our own way, never truly knowing whether we are right or wrong. We learn how to show emotions that have different vibrations and these skills are difficult; very individual in their nature, so life can be complex as each one of us develops communication skills - hoping that they are the correct way of conducting and expressing ourselves.

We are not able to take back any word form once it has been spoken, and this fact can have a devastating affect on others and even on our own minds, if the words are not spoken in a positive way.

We are entering into a time where a new level of knowledge of each other can be explored and can hopefully produce another approach to our deep inner self that needs reassurance and understanding.

This will hopefully enable us to resolve our differences in such a way that the need for enlightenment will bring the human race together, ready to travel and enjoy the exciting new era that can be full of enrichment. This will hopefully unify us all towards a far greater understanding.

Life teaches us that we must learn by our own mistakes, but we make so many along the way that we may come to see our life as one big mistake. But, over the last two decades, a new optimism has been reshaping our thoughts and a deeper realisation is dawning - we have been born with empowerment and we will finally create a better world because we have realised the reason why we are here on earth.

The answer was in our hearts all along!

Finding the answer has entailed travelling through a maze of emotions. But, even though the journey has been amazing, we return to the one truth – found in the thing that created us all in the very beginning - the seed of love.

If we could just learn to share the flame of unconditional love and shed light - even in the darkest corners of our minds - we would only need to radiate the light that reflects from our universe to light up our souls.

It would shed light on our pathways throughout all of our lifetimes.

This was never meant to be a dark life. We all share the light provided by the sun and moon.

How different it could have been without both lights showing us the way.

Our eyes see many things, some light, some dark, but if we stand strong in our own belief and can find the strength to stay positive and learn the integral skills required, we can begin to understand the difference in all of our emotional fields.

This knowledge will give the human race a true vision as to how unified we really are.

We are also very capable of developing the emotional skill that we need to maintain and keep our inner flame of love and life aglow.

*

The power of life is the rugged rock protruding from a stream; the stream flows round it.

Tenderness

Tenderness is an expression of deep love and it is full of compassion and grace. It has within itself a great understanding of life and can be generated through the heat of one's hand. The touch of a tender person renders you without passion but it pulsates below the surface, creating a sense of well-being.

The flow is natural, helping you to relax, and feel the energy connecting and releasing its flow. So beautiful is the feeling that your skin starts to glow; feeling like a bird's feather stroking gently against the skin; releasing the natural flow and essence that rises from deep within. You experience a feeling of great comfort, similar to when your mother's arms cradled you as a child, allowing your body to drift gently into sleep as she rocked you back and forth. As she touched your cheek you snuggled ever deeper into the warmth of her embrace.

When your father lifted you high, your hands reached out, as if to touch the sky, trusting him with a chuckle that lit up your whole face, enjoying the moment. You had faith in him.

When a gentle smile from another lights up their eyes you are receiving a gift that has no price.

It costs you nothing to be nice and, as love rises from the well of your heart, you must find a way to pass on this wondrous gift. Channelling its wealth of knowledge through the open space of your heart may take a brief moment, but people's memories are long and they will always remember when you came into their lives.

Always think of the kind heart that helped you in your moment of need when you express caring words of encouragement to another, it will mean more to them than you will ever believe.

Some people find it difficult to show their feelings, it's true, but I am sure that they will never ever forget you.

So be tender to yourself, learn from it and you will see that life can be so bountiful - once you believe.

Let that wonderful energy flow and be honest, open and true, because that wonderful tenderness exists deep within you.

Respect

Why do you need respect from another person?

Is it to confirm what you feel about yourself or to feel superior to the other?

When you are of the correct nature you are already receiving respect and exchanging a mutual understanding of how to be; confirming that all is equal.

Once you enter the sphere of "all there is" you have overcome your own actions towards others, so now you can walk and be in the essence of time and that can and will give you the freedom to overcome past experiences.

Doubt

Am I on the right pathway?

You will have doubts about the choices that you make, but stay focused, try not to give into thoughts that have no foundation because these may leave you feeling full of regret.

Try to stay centred when making decisions and, if in doubt, ask someone you trust to help you.

Your future is important to you, and those closest to you. Depending on what you have in mind to assist you in your future be assured that you will make the right choices if you believe in yourself enough.

You must have this knowledge in your heart before you proceed onto the next stage.

This may not be immediate, you may have to be patient for the process to develop, but be ever mindful that what happens throughout your life is all part of the ever deeper wisdom that you, as a person, are and will be in the future.

Pure Thoughts

Pure thoughts are a natural flow of well-being.

As they leave your mind they are full of love and compassion.

Emotional and gentle thoughts towards others are calming and nurturing.

They bring about change in another's reactions as they pulsate from one to another.

They bring peace where once there was conflict.

They cleanse the mind of negative thoughts that pollute.

Your flow of thoughts are connected to your inner emotions. Another person may have a different outlook on life that can bring about unwanted thoughts, this can be very demanding on your own inner being. You may ask yourself how to keep your own thoughts under control and not to be tempted into a cascade of negative thoughts. Your will power can be sorely tested at this point, but try not to be drawn into a conflict of interests, just be aware of your own harmonious levels, in which you desire to live your life.

Try to keep your thought forms of a pure nature; others may try to change your thoughts for their own selfish desires.

When the desire is to change another this may have a devastating effect on your own life and any other person's to whom your thoughts may be directed, the fast acting flow of thoughts will always find their destination.

To restore balance to your thoughts as quickly as possible, before they start to bring about discontent within yourself, be good-natured towards others. This can act like a balm to the soul, ensuring another person's happiness.

When you do this you show that you have the understanding of what it takes to live alongside each other.

Therefore, being connected with your very own thoughts will help to empower you and enable you to overcome any unwanted influences that you may encounter throughout your life.

Power

Power is a word that carries with it a feeling of struggle.

We feel that we must show confidence to become all-powerful and overcome whatever discord affects our own understanding of truth.

But these feelings can become distorted over a period of time.

When we have power we have the means to overcome all adversity and it is from pure strength that we feel the need to link to other selves that can help access and possibly share all of the powerful feelings that lay deep within ourselves.

These feelings of power are only powerful when accompanied by the truth.

This then is the key – with truth and power combined we can develop an energy force that is purely for the greater good of mankind.

When we step into the realms of the greater good we have succeeded in overthrowing the influences that have tried to undermine us as a human race.

There are so many advantages in walking free and beginning a life that is full and which is built on a much stronger foundation.

Our stress emotion will now no longer have the monopoly over us - because our souls have the pleasure of living and breathing thoughts of a kind that can and will give us a sense of purpose - that will hear the bells ringing out the changes for mankind.

So is it possible to be able to link into the heart of our own truth?

To allow the powerful gifts from our own inner strengths to be able to evolve?

Can we allow hope to flourish within each and every one of us?

You will know by now that the answer to all of these questions is a resounding **YES**!

Strength

Strength is our very own inner vortex.

It is an unseen energy that gathers in power and energises us when we need to overcome any adversity or when we may feel vulnerable.

When we allow fear to be part of the structure of our vortex, every negative thought drains our energy system.

Our thoughts are the key to keeping our own strengths in check.

Any project that we may be considering may require more strength and energy, and that acknowledgement may give us a sense that we do not have enough self-worth.

Thoughts that help us to overcome a lack of self-esteem or confidence will help us through many parts of our life. These parts are just like streams and rivers. Some experiences need more thought than others. A stream represents one way of thinking, as it is slow, easy and enjoyable; meaning that we have taken a rest from our normal everyday thought pattern. In this way our energies build up, restoring balance and preparing us for the more difficult parts of the project that need more careful planning.

All of these stages ensure that we are aware of more demanding parts of the process – but we will be prepared for the challenge.

Each time we undertake to discover our capabilities we are building up our strength, not just our physical strength but also our mental abilities. Possessing both of these can have an amazing effect on our emotions. Life can be like a stream, river or even a torrent and we can never be quite aware of the vast distance that we have covered.

Life can stretch before us like an endless stream but we have to overcome adversity of thought, which is ourself requesting the inner self to undergo another challenge. This is okay, but if we allow our lower thoughts to take us into the realms of fear we will find ourselves abandoning the project that was so dear to us; leaving us with a sense of weakness.

Life moves on and our feelings may be at their lowest ebb, as we allowed our thoughts to influence us enough to abandon any new experience.

We may also feel at a disadvantage as our strength is being put to the test.

At this point it would be good to take the time to stop and take a few deep breaths, because this is not a race against time - it is just our lives in motion.

We can always attempt to take up the challenge if and when it feels right again. It might take many attempts, but as long as we keep going, we will eventually have a far deeper understanding of what we can achieve.

All of these contributions carry us towards whatever we choose to do, whether large or small tasks, and whatever will have a far greater meaning long term. They also provide us with an abundance of our own inner strengths.

Producing more positive thinking enables us to move on with the understanding that we have not let ourselves down.

When we arrive at certain times we must look back and reminisce at many unexplained happenings. We may begin to notice and feel that some form of synchronicity may have been moving around and alongside us - just like a stream of ideas meandering through our everyday thoughts and feelings.

When we are at peace, we can concentrate on our self-reflection and what looks like our own image appears in the mirror of glass or on calm, still waters.

But life is constantly on the move and likewise we may feel a stirring within us to keep moving as the river of life beckons and it has so much more to offer.

So, we make choices whether to wade in or not, knowing that once we make our decision, we must be prepared for the adventures that life will throw at us.

Be ever mindful that at any stage of our lives the apparition of fear can surface and appear to be testing our true sense of purpose, so it is important to find inner will and continue to be truly adventurous.

Honour your own sense of commitment - and every journey that you may wish to undertake will be smoother.

We must be resolved throughout and stay focused, all the while building up our very own internal strength.

This can take a lot of energy but once we have recognised and realised the balance between each of these stages, we then give ourselves freely into metamorphosis and find the time for our full concentration.

We are always working towards a different level of understanding and we will find that our lives become more finely tuned, working with our strengths, ever focusing on the outcome of each experience we endeavour to undertake.

*

Your family are your support system, until you decide to let go.

Laughter

Laughter is the most uplifting of all our emotions as it holds within itself a moving biography of thought and memory.

We have the ability to bring great joy to all of those who share our lives, and to be able to laugh is to be part of the truest essence of the many great humanitarian changes being realised in the world.

Anyone who undertakes to share this amazing energy with charisma and expertise, elects to bring great happiness to us all - although there may be times when this can be at the total detriment to themselves.

When mixed with tears, laughter can begin a healing process that can help us through any part of our life that has held us captive for too long

Deep within our emotions we will find a sense of being free from those times that have left us with a deep sense of *not belonging*.

To many people, giggling may signal a sign of disrespect but for many it can be a way of releasing any disharmony or embarrassment felt by the other.

There are many reasons why laughter can be present in any situation, ultimately it is off-set by any familiarity that exists between us as we undergo similar experiences – in this way it draws us into a shared and very distinctive emotion.

Relationships

Life must still go on, even when a relationship has become impossible to maintain.

The first knowledge of other people begins in early life, when we undergo varying stages of growth; watching and learning as adults go through many forms of relationships with their peers.

We also see how life can be manipulating as we slowly get drawn into the lives of our early stage mentors. Although we have no way of knowing that - later on in life - these first stages of our growth will have a lasting effect on our choices.

As life progresses, we build some friendships that may last a lifetime, while some may fade.

When we reach puberty a different emotion starts to evolve. We start to attract the same or opposite gender and that can lead to all sorts of misunderstandings and emotional furrows. We sometimes need to have advice from professional people who understand what we are going through.

Emotional attraction in the early stages of adult life is also demanding on the many thoughts we have in regards to ourselves. We become a very good critic of our many *levels of self.*

Other people influence us and that plays a major part in how we conduct ourselves.

The next stages of life are taken up with finding a suitable relationship that will give us the most joy and happiness. This is by far the most important part of the emotional *free zone*.

Everyone remembers their first love or crush – and this first encounter with the love energy is by far the most poignant. The emotion is comforting and has no hidden agenda. It is possible to move on from this without any unwanted conflictions of emotions, but the desire to feel attracted by another becomes stronger and we might then enter into the realms of love that will carry us on through life.

When couples first form a relationship they will always retain the memories of when they first felt any emotion towards each other. One or both of them will believe that they have found a partnership that will have a solid, lifelong foundation but these emotions can be overwhelming and completely take over - this is termed as *love sickness* because anything else of importance seems to fade into the background. The desire to spend every moment with the person who has captivated our heart is immense.

This emotion though can be disabling and destructive.

Many have fallen into the trap of giving up their lives to be with their loved one – this, at first, may be thought of as romantic as each explores the other's potential.

It is important though to remember that we are all individuals as well and we must still continue to pursue our own dreams.

A true relationship should be one of equal encouragement.

If, on the other hand, one person starts to become negative then the relationship starts to malfunction and these emotional difficulties can have a long-lasting effect; what was once a happy experience has now become a battle of wills to determine who was at fault.

Both people then become victims of their own natures.

There is no right or wrong way to build a relationship. It evolves between two people as they create the environment that is right for them to grow in. Their decisions are theirs alone, but both need to feel that they are living in an environment that has equal opportunities and that they are both appreciated and thanked for their efforts.

But equally there are other reasons as to why relationships come to an end, as there are no guarantees as to how long they should last. It would be well to see them in a different light: i.e. they are there just for your individual growth.

Have you outgrown the other person?

Are they no longer inspirational in your life?

Is your life requesting that you part, to enable each of you to reclaim the life that you desire?

There are no hard and fast answers as to why the human race is constantly searching for a deep-rooted love. As part of the evolution of man it is seen as part of the cycle of life to be in love. But this could mean that we need to live our lives in love with life itself.

This energy is the fruit from which all else can grow, so that all relationships can be nurtured.

We are constantly learning and evolving as human beings and have been given a responsibility towards each other. There are deep underlying issues in our understanding of each other that show the flaws in our emotional fields and these have a large impact on our lives.

Life is like a jigsaw - it is made up of many parts. If we can truly begin to understand the true meaning of the many happenings that we undergo - that have a massive impact on our emotions on a daily basis - then we are on the road to truly discovering who we really are.

We are like motor vehicles moving in the flow of time, the destination is sometimes unknown and we also may expect others to fit their lives around our plans, but initially this is in our self-interest.

As another piece of our jigsaw is put into place, relationships are a constant part of our growth. Regardless of capacity, they begin from birth and continue throughout one's life, they all have a long-lasting affect on our emotions.

Learning to live alongside each other can be a tremendous task as we have to accept another's ways and that can be very demanding and very tiring, unless the energy being shared is of a loving nature.

This ethos can bring about harmony and uplift us all – but this is not always possible as emotions can also bring displeasure and discord and these jigsaw pieces have to be addressed as part of the learning curve towards self-realisation.

Knowing thyself can only be derived by accepting that we begin life as a fragile human being who has deep feelings.

We also need to realise that the art of finding ourselves is through the understanding found whilst in relationships. In this way we ponder on our own growth and that is all part of the active part of ourselves becoming whole. This process can take a lot of effort as we need to find the strength to overcome adversity and this is not always the easiest of things to do, especially if we feel that we are being victimised by people.

If at these junctures of life we can just know that these moments do pass, they are not meant to dominate our emotions for a lifetime and also know that they are happening to help us to assess our evolution then our strength should be paramount.

We should not seek to overpower others but to empower ourselves.

This can only have a lasting effect in helping to build lifelong, stable relationships - and in helping others understand their life path too.

*

Destiny is a precursor of all life.

Evaluate The Meaning
Of Truth

Truth has great meaning in our everyday life. It is a powerful energy with a sense of purpose.

When truth is present in any situation it empowers.

It is magnetic and has a wonderful quality of reassurance.

In the company of others, truth encourages peace and harmony, and it shows in the ways that others respond to you; allowing trust to develop.

One is able to be oneself without fear or prejudice.

When words are spoken in a truthful way they resonate and inspire confidence.

They can also have an impact on any unhealthy situations that may have developed through any misuse in the development of relationships and when another person confesses about their involvement in detrimental actions it can begin a process of emotional healing.

Truthful words are abundant. They have a wonderful quality and can be repeated over and over again. They make all things possible and bring humour and dynamics to the human race.

Truth is a living energy so it also evolves with time; what may have been seen as the truth at one stage of any person's growth may take on a different meaning afterwards, but the underlying factor will always be present.

As long as the goal is honest in thought and deed, then all things can be at peace.

Daydreaming Is A Form Of Meditation

Daydreaming and meditation are both connected to the inner person and they allow you to visualise yourself in different situations.

They are viewed by many as practices of peaceful contemplation.

They may bring about changes in stressful situations, encouraging you to discover ways to overcome anxiety and indecision.

Meditation has been used for centuries by gifted souls who recognise the benefits of being in a tranquil state of quietness; a slow internal massage that has a soothing affect on the mind, allowing oneself to be relaxed in mind, body and spirit.

It is also an integral part of many whose beliefs encourage them to use meditation as a spiritual practice in order to lift the many different vibrations on earth.

When all things are linked by positive thought energy, it is of great importance to future generations.

We can connect to our higher, positive thoughts bringing about change within ourselves, and, by doing so, play an important role for these generations who have yet to discover their true potential and what effect they will have on each other. They are of great importance, developing minds that will benefit all mankind.

They are already a major connection in the worlds consciousness, bringing people together in groups where their energy can be of benefit to all concerned. This encourages the positive thought vibration into our existence and can possibly bring changes to how we perceive all things.

Looking deeply into one's own actions can have a marked affect on the way that we think, this will hopefully bring about a deeper understanding of our evolving world.

Incorporating some quiet time into what may be a very demanding life, can have a tremendous impact on our own ability and strengths, helping us to overcome any unwanted thoughts or feelings that can be disabling and destructive. Our own energy has, within itself, the empowerment to help us and others overcome any form of adversity.

Throughout our lifetime we will be called upon by our own inner being to grow.

At these times we will be sorely tested in regards to our own nature, searching for the inner strength to uphold our core beliefs. Our true inner strengths will support and guide us, correcting any indecision in our thoughts and feelings.

These moments are when our own inner teacher requires our attention.

Listen carefully to your *inner voice* and let the voice (your own intuition) be there for you.

When we take the time to be with ourselves in quiet contemplation, the realisation that all things are possible begins to take shape in our mind.

Material Desires

When in the stages of material desire, the need for want is uppermost in one's mind. It is paramount to the individual who believes that the only way to achieve anything is to be financially wealthy.

These thoughts have had a large impact on the human race and its emotions and, as a result, we are now in total discord.

Not all attainments have been achieved through wealth though. True knowledge comes through diligence and hard work and the reward is attainment and recognition – both of which can have a deep and long-lasting affect.

These attainments can be passed from generation to generation.

When in full flight, the creative thought energy will be unleashed to enable another wondrous moment of inventiveness to evolve.

These moments are born into history and have been ongoing for centuries.

Some great artists were born into impoverished conditions, but they honed their craft, becoming adept, although they were not always famous in their lifetime.

They have all shown the world that greatness is born from within and they allowed their emotional intellect to bring the desired outcome into their lives.

We cannot buy emotions - they are kept deep inside of ourselves. Sometimes, the smallest act of kindness can bring the greatest of pleasures, especially where there is no financial gain.

How many persons have been given a gift only to be overwhelmed with emotion when learning of its true meaning? These emotional links that have been proven over and over again are deeply profound.

As history informs us, too much wealth has been known to also have devastating effects on some individuals who have no understanding of the power it has over the emotions. For example, their wealth may be taken from them suddenly, and then their emotions suffer.

Wealth can primarily be used for the greater good of all, and is shown to be beneficial to those who are not privileged so that they may enhance their life.

But being aware of our true potential should be paramount in our mind. To be able to help ourself become the truest possible person we can be - with or without financial assistance – should be our goal.

Colours - Sounds - Scents

These are vivid and play an integral part in our everyday lives. Our emotions are highly charged by colours and they help form and inform the deep knowing within us all.

We are aware of the impact of colours. They induce deep feelings and memories that interact with the threads of our life tapestry. We are attracted to colours and bring them into our daily lives. They enhance our emotional well-being.

There has been a great deal of research into how our moods are affected by colours – they are so beneficial to our energy systems.

Colours can calm us and enliven us as well. In some cases, just thinking of a colour can have the fastest acting response to our disquiet and we are finally able to find some peaceful time - just a few minutes can be all that we need. We can then be still and slowly let the colour or colours unfold and seep into our very hearts.

We all have a connective understanding of any form of music.

Music has always been used as a messaging system, and deep within its structure are metaphors that connect to our innermost emotional core. We are able to be deeply moved by the phrasing of the lyrics and the musical score.

When we are able to recognise our responses to different sounds we are inadvertently responding to a deep, primitive need to move our physical bodies and release any pent up emotional feelings. These emotional movements are a way of releasing and removing the barriers that keep us contained in an otherwise streamlined existence. To be able to dance and sway is a natural human response. It is being at one with nature.

To be able to dance, jog, exercise or just to be able to move gracefully is all part of our natural way.

Being in the rhythmic essence can bring enchantment and a pure state of exhilaration to those who appreciate these wonderful levels of musical genius.

Music brings deep peace to the most troubled of souls.

One of our greatest gifts is the sense of smell; we are privileged to be informed by this natural gift. It can enhance life in dramatic ways and it can also have a profound affect on our emotions.

We are not always aware of our reaction towards certain smells, but we know that they have an effect on our emotions and, if not recognised, can bring thoughts into focus that would otherwise have lain dormant.

There is association in all things, especially the senses; they are all entwined as gifts for us in our wonderful growth.

When all of our gifts are used together they can bring a sense of great pleasure.

Without our senses, life would be quite barren. For anyone who has suffered sight or hearing problems, the senses of smell and taste will always be considered a great gift.

When our lives are enhanced by the gift of sense and the thrill of scent – then we are truly aware that all things are possible.

Be assured that I have also undergone this journey.

It has taken the whole of my lifetime to form this profound sense of knowing.

I feel blessed to have undergone such a journey, although, at times, never knowing from whence I have summoned the strength to continue, but I have now found a deep sense of self.

No longer am I in the dark with regards to myself, but I savour the light, as it shows me the way.

I pay homage to everyone who has shared my life because without them I could never have found the courage just to "be".

I trust that everything is just as it should be in my life and I hope to continue to explore whatever life has to teach me; to meet the people that I am meant to meet and to, hopefully, add to my knowledge.

The Author, Carol Allgood, can be contacted via her email address:

dont.sufferinsilence@live.co.uk

Lightning Source UK Ltd.
Milton Keynes UK
UKOW050128200712

196256UK00001B/33/P